PIONEER VA   ESS, INC

TENNIS

SEAN FINNIGAN

Tennis is a sport.

Here are two tennis players.

They are playing tennis.

You need a tennis ball
and a **racket**
to play tennis.
Here is a tennis racket.

Here is a tennis ball.
The ball is made of rubber.
It is covered with soft **felt**.

Tennis is played on a **court**.
A net goes across the court.

One player stands
on one side of the net.
The other player stands
on the other side of the net.
One player is the **server**.
The other player
is the **receiver**.

A server hits the ball
over the net
to the receiver.

Two players can play
as a team.
They hit the ball
to the other team
of two players.
This is called playing **doubles**.

Tennis is a fun sport that is played all over the world.

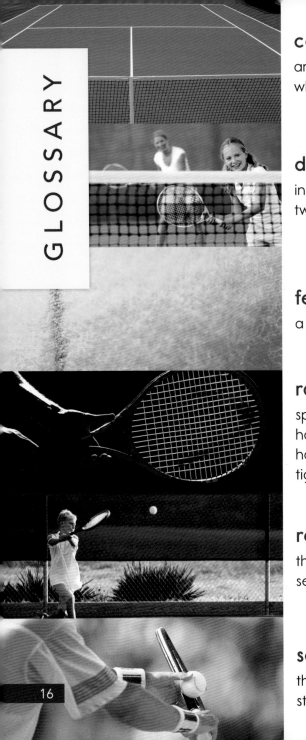

court

an area marked with lines where sports are played

doubles

in tennis, to play with teams of two players

felt

a soft, non-woven fibrous cloth

racket

sporting equipment with a handled frame and an open hoop with cord stretched tightly across

receiver

the player who receives the served ball

server

the player who hits the ball to start the play in a game